PARAMETERS OF IRISH
IN ENGLISH

A. Norman Jeffares

PARAMETERS OF IRISH LITERATURE IN ENGLISH

A lecture given at the Princess Grace
Irish Library

on

Friday 25 April 1986 at 8.00 p.m.

COLIN SMYTHE
Gerrards Cross, 1986

Copyright © 1986 The Princess Grace Irish Library

First published for The Princess Grace Irish Library
by Colin Smythe Limited, Gerrards Cross, Buckinghamshire

ISBN 0–86140–246—4

Acknowledgement is made to Macmillan London Ltd
for permission to quote Yeats's 'The Mermaid'.

Produced in Great Britain
Set by Grove Graphics, Tring, Herts
Printed by Billing & Sons Ltd, Worcester

Parameters of Irish Literature in English

Ireland is a small country with a large literary achievement. The tradition goes back into the mists of mythology with stories about the Tuatha da Danann, the tribes of the Goddess Dana, an ancient divine race who occupied Ireland before the Celts came to the island. Irish literature was largely oral but we do know that books were being written a century before St Patrick brought Christianity to Ireland, when he arrived in 432 AD. He found a flourishing literary world: druids, poets and antiquarians were men of considerable status and influence in the aristocratic society of Ireland. Kings, powerful families and individual learned men kept large manuscript books, often beautifully illuminated, and the Christian monasteries followed suit, the monks in their scriptoria copying the gospels *and* the pagan literature as well.

Many of these manuscript books were destroyed in the dark period of the Danish invasions which devastated the country from the close of the eighth century until the Battle of Clontarf in 1014, others during the warfare that followed on the Anglo–Norman invasion of 1169, and yet more were lost in the suppression of the monasteries in the sixteenth century.

What we have of the old pagan Irish literature is largely preserved in the surviving medieval manuscript books. For instance, the twelfth century *Book of the Dun Cow* and the *Book of Leinster* and the fifteenth century *Yellow Book of Lecan* are the main sources for the best known of the Ulster cycle of epic tales, *The Tain Bo Cualgne*, which dates back to the eighth century in its language, while some of its poetry is probably two centuries older.

The material of this Gaelic epic has had its effect on modern Ireland — Pearse, the bilingual poet who was one of the leaders of the 1916 rising which led to the foundation of the twenty-six county republic of Ireland and the six county province of Northern Ireland, made 'a cult' of Cuchulain, the hero of the *Tain*. And he was led to this heroic material because of the interest in Gaelic literature which had begun in the late eighteenth century and developed increasingly in the nineteenth century in Ireland. It found expression in the work of devoted scholars and translators as well as in the writings of such authors as, say, the intense and eccentric poet James Clarence Mangan, of the sterner Sir Samuel Ferguson, a translator true to his original Irish material, of the exuberant story-teller Standish O'Grady, of Douglas Hyde, whose *Love Songs of Connacht* (1893) so fitly accompanied his founding the Gaelic League in 1893 and becoming Ireland's first President in 1938, of Yeats who largely created the Celtic Twilight and through the Abbey Theatre turned it into a more effective Irish Renaissance, of AE the visionary, of Lady Gregory and of Synge — to name but a few of them. And today we have in addition to the poems and plays in which Yeats made this saga material known, and to Lady Gregory's translations, a fine contemporary translation of the *Tain* by Thomas Kinsella, beautifully illustrated, incidentally, by an Irish artist, Louis Le Brocquy.

So, then, Cuchulain, Emer his wife and Eithne his mistress, King Conor of Ulster, and Deirdre of the Sorrows whose lover, Naoise Conor killed along with his brothers Ainnle and Ardan, Fergus, Conor's predecessor, and Maeve of Connaught as well as the all too human Irish gods and goddesses are now deeply imprinted on the Irish consciousness — and on many a mind in many other countries where English is spoken or read. And there are, of course, many other characters and tales. Besides the Ulster cycle there is the Fenian, stories centring upon the king Finn MacCool, his wife Grainne who ran away with Dermot, and his son Oisin who wandered with the fairy princess Niamh through three enchanted islands, though three hundred years of time before returning to an Ireland where St Patrick's Christianity now held sway.

It is perhaps paradoxical that the pagan literature was preserved by monks in monasteries, but that is typical. In considering Irish literature written in English — to mention but a few of its names, it is the literature of Swift, the supreme satirist, of Berkeley, the Bishop of Cloyne, the idealist philosopher, of Edmund Burke, the conservative political philosopher, of Oscar Wilde, the wit and dandy, of George Bernard Shaw, the socialist propagandist and playwright, of Yeats, the leading poet, and of Joyce, the leading novelist of our age — we cannot dismiss or neglect this old Irish literature that the great manuscript books preserved. We cannot ignore the oral traditions that survive, some of them to this day. Literature in Irish has been a blending of past and present, or oral and written literature, just as there is a blended history behind the language used in Ireland — Irish itself, then a dash of Danish around the coastal towns, followed by Norman French and medieval English — and finally an English which has been affected by all those elements.

It is with the literature written in English that we are primarily concerned. Those eighteenth, nineteenth and twentieth century Irish writers I have mentioned will be found, like many more, in histories of English literature. They are assimilated there — like the Americans Henry James or T. S. Eliot — but they should also be considered within the history of Irish literature. All of them were born in Ireland, educated there, in effect shaped as writers there before they left the island to make their livings elsewhere.

They are better understood within the history of their own culture. Their backgrounds are different; they grew up in a country utterly unlike England, unlike Europe, unlike America. This is the result of Ireland's geographical position and her history: of invasions: of the clash — which continues — between Christian and pagan ideas, of the survival of the traditions of an older Irish-speaking civilisation in oral literature, of the seventeenth century struggle between Catholic and Protestant, of many rebellions and risings against English rule, of the nineteenth century's establishment of a scheme of national education which made the island English-speaking, of the twentieth century's emergence of the Republic of Ireland as a full nation state with as its northern neighbour an uneasy Ulster.

All this often complex history has, inevitably, affected Irish writers and the very varied literature they have created. The Princess Grace Irish Library is a most welcome centre, because it will offer readers and, above all, researchers a magnificent opportunity to see this Irish literature in perspective. By publishing the results of their scholarly research and criticism researchers will affect future views of the achievement of Irish literature. Specialised studies show us more and more about particular Irish authors but they need to be based upon an awareness not only of how writers interact with each other[1] but how they react to their own times and the traditions that have made them what they are.

The first great Irish writer in English[2] was Jonathan Swift, the

Dean of St Patrick's, master of irony, and of the *saeva indignatio*, the fierce anger that inspired his satires. *Gulliver's Travels* is an attack upon human pride. The King of the Brobdingnagians, the giants, is horrified by Gulliver's account of European politics: 'the Bulk of your Natives', he concludes, are 'the most pernicious Race of little Odious Vermin that Nature ever suffered to crawl upon the Surface of the Earth'. But *Gulliver's Travels* is also vastly entertaining and children still enjoy its Lilliputians, its flying island, and its philosophical Hounyhnhnms and bestial Yahoos. Swift had an irrepressible sense of wit as his 'Verses on the Death of Dr Swift' remind us:

> My female Friends, whose tender Hearts
> Have better learn'd to act their Parts,
> Receive the News in *doleful Dumps*,
> 'The Dean is dead, (*and what is Trumps?*)
> 'Then Lord have Mercy on his Soul.
> '(Ladies I'll venture for the *Vole*.)
> "Six Deans they say must bear the Pall.
> '(I wish I knew what *King* to call.)
> 'Madam, your Husband will attend
> 'The Funeral of so good a Friend.
> 'No Madam, 'tis a shocking Sight,
> 'And he's engag'd To-morrow Night!
> 'My Lady Club wou'd take it ill,
> 'If he shou'd fail her at *Quadrill.*
> 'He lov'd the Dean. (*I lead a Heart.*)
> 'But dearest Friends, they say, must part.
> 'His Time was come, he ran his Race;
> 'We hope he's in a better Place.' ...
>
> 'He gave the little Wealth he had,
> 'To build a House for Fools and Mad:
> 'And shew'd by one satyric Touch,
> 'No Nation wanted it so much:
> 'That Kingdom he hath left his Debtor,
> 'I wish it soon may have a Better.'

Swift, however, can also be regarded in the context of Irish literature — and history — as the first powerfully articulate anti-colonialist author.[3] 'Burn everything English but their coal', he said, for he resented the encroachment of the Parliament of

Westminster upon what ought to have been the terrain of the Parliament of Dublin :

> Were not the people of Ireland born as Free as those of England? How have they forfeited their Freedom? Is not their Parliament as fair a Representative of the People as that of England? And hath not their Privy Council as great or a greater share in the Administration of Publick Affairs? Are they not Subjects of the same King? Does not the same Sun shine on them? Have they not the same God for their Protector? Am I a Free-Man in England, and do I become a Slave in six Hours by crossing the Channel?

By crossing the channel Swift was returning to an Ireland whose poverty enraged him into writing *A Modest Proposal for Preventing the Children of the Poor in Ireland from being Burdensome and for making them Beneficial* (1729). This proposal is put forward in a matter-of-fact way as though some social economist was writing it; its outrageous solution is apparently advanced dispassionately and this has the greater effect on us :

> I have been assured by a very knowing American of my Acquaintance in London; that a young healthy Child; well nursed, is at a Year old, a most delicious, nourishing and wholesome Food : whether Stewed, Roasted, Baked or Boiled; and, I make no doubt, that it will equally serve in a Fricasie or Ragoust.

The calculations are carefully made by the proposer, who argues that, out of a total of 120,00 children, 20,000 could be reserved for breeding and the remaining 100,000 sold when a year old 'to Persons of Quality and Fortune, through the Kingdom; always advising the Mothers to let them suck plentifully in the last month, so as to render them plump and fat for a good Table'. Swift's *saeva indignatio* had reached its most savage point. 'I grant', remarks his proposer, 'this food will be somewhat dear, and therefore very proper for Landlords; who, as they have already devoured most of the parents, seem to have the best title to the children'.

Swift is the first of the four eighteenth century Irish authors whom the poet Yeats celebrated. During the time that he was a Senator of the Irish Free State (this was the period when he won the Nobel Prize for Literature) he began to think that the eighteenth century was the one orderly period in Irish history — 'that one Irish century', he said, 'that escaped from darkness and confusion'[4]. He chose, however, only four people, four authors, to represent the achievement of the eighteenth century. In his poem 'Blood and the Moon' he saw these four as his own symbolic literary and spiritual ancestors:

> I declare this tower is my symbol; I declare
> This winding, gyring, spiring treadmill of a stair is
>   My ancestral stair;
>
> That Goldsmith and the Dean, Berkeley and Burke have
>   travelled there.

In another poem, 'The Seven Sages', he celebrated them again, this time as his political predecessors, admitting them — or, rather, compelling them — into agreement with his own views:

> Whether they knew it or not,
> Goldsmith and Burke, Swift and the Bishop of Cloyne
> All hated Whiggery; but what is Whiggery?
> A levelling, rancorous, rational sort of mind
> That never looked out of the eye of a saint
>   Or out of drunkard's eye.

A poet concentrates upon, intensifies, and illuminates. We do not expect him necessarily to give us a balanced view of a century's writing — he might be a dull dog if he did. But we do need sometimes to question or to gloss. What other Irish writers were there in the eighteenth century besides the four upon whom Yeats concentrated? The fact that Yeats added to Dean Swift, Bishop Berkeley and Edmund Burke, Oliver Goldsmith, the author of *She Stoops to Conquer*, a comedy still popular today, suggests that we should look at other Irish dramatists who, like Goldsmith, found their audiences overseas.

The first impressive figure among them is Nahum Tate (1652–1715); notorious for creating a version of *King Lear* with a happy ending, he wrote the libretto of Purcell's *Dido and Aeneas*, became Poet Laureate and collaborated with Nicholas Brady, another Irishman, in their famous metrical version of the psalms. He wrote *Panacea — a Poem on Tea*, and I still remember my father singing me to sleep as a very young child with Tate's 'While Shepherds watched their flocks by night' and 'As pants the Hart for cooling streams'.

One of the quirks of literary reputation is the general neglect of Thomas Southerne (1660–1746); eight years younger than Nahum Tate, he managed his financial affairs in London better than Tate, who had to hide from his creditors in the Royal Mint. Pope paid tribute to Southerne's success :

> Tom whom Heaven sent down to raise
> The price of prologues and of plays

And Southerne's plays are eminently worth reviving now, not just his *Oroonoko* (1695) founded on Mrs Behn's novel of that name, but such risqué comedies as *The Disappointment* (1684), *Sir Anthony Love* (1690) — which I hope will shortly be in print again, for it is likely to be published by Cadenus Press in Dublin — *The Wife's Excuse: or Cuckolds make themselves* (1692), and *The Maid's Last Prayer or, Any rather than fail* (1693). These are plays in which Southerne based his satire upon the vagaries and affectations of that fashionable aristocratic London society, in which he himself moved with ease, with a sharp observation and a keen psychological insight which should attract modern audiences.

Congreve, whether he was born in Yorkshire in 1670 or, as some Irish critics have it, earlier in Ireland, was an Irish wit, educated in Ireland, like Swift attending Kilkenny College and then Trinity College Dublin. His plays certainly marked the height of Restoration comedy and are still staged most successfully. *Love for Love* (1695) is a sparkling romp and perhaps a better stage play than *The Way of the World* (1700) which, though many now regard it as the supreme achievement of the comedy of wit, was not to the taste of its time.

The new style of comedy which succeeded it was a gentler one, though no less sparkling. And it was another Irish writer, George Farquhar, who is reputed to have fought at the Battle of the Boyne at the tender age of thirteen, who moved the scenes of his most successful comedies out of London to the provinces. *The Recruiting Officer* (1706) and *The Beaux Stratagem* (1707) still captivate audiences by their pace, their exuberance, their dialogue and situations; but they portray a wider range of society than the earlier plays which were centred on 'the Town', its attitudinising and immoral cynicism; they do this very amusingly indeed and with more tolerance for the foibles of their characters than had been shown in their predecessors. Susanna Centlivre (1670–1723), for instance, Congreve's contemporary, wrote somewhat slighter plays of intrigue in the same style as Farquhar; she had run away from home and met a Cambridge undergraduate who dressed her as a boy and kept her at Cambridge until he could afford to send her to London. She was obviously an attractive girl: twice widowed by twenty, she married a third time in 1706 and then decided to give up acting, concentrating instead upon writing such plays as *The Wonder! A Woman keeps a Secret* (1714) and *A Bold Stroke for a Wife* (1718).

Comedy veered firmly into sentimentality with Sir Richard Steele, in his play *The Conscious Lovers* (1722). He appealed to middle class audiences in the theatres, he even praised city merchants, who used to be a butt for earlier dramatists. Steele, now better known for his essays in the *Tatler* and the *Spectator*, and later in *The Guardian* and *The Englishman*, was, like Swift, a supreme shaper of public opinion in England where he had arrived at the age of thirteen, and where, having lost an estate in Wexford by enlisting in the Coldstream Guards, he made his life.

In the latter part of the eighteenth century a large colony of Irish dramatists was successfully busy in London. Among them was Charles Macklin, an actor with energy matching that of David Garrick. He killed a fellow actor in a green room fight and got away with it; he was still acting at eighty, having written many plays including *Love a la Mode* (produced 1759; published 1784), a lively comedy. Like his *The True Born Irishman*; or, *The Irish Fine Lady* (1762; rewritten as *The Irish Fine Lady*, 1767) and *The Man of the World* (1781), it is well worth reviving, for Macklin breathed fresh life into stock comic plots through good dialogue. The speeches of his army officer Sir Callaghan O'Brallagan, for instance, are amusingly idiosynscratic. And he can be realistic, too, when he is asked to describe a battle:

> ... it rebuts a man of honour to be talking to ladies of battles, and sieges, and skrimages — it looks like gasconading and making the fanfaron. Besides, madam, I give you my honour, there is no such thing in nature as making a true description of a battle.

CHARLOTTE: How so, sir?

SIR CALLAGHAN: Why, madam, there is much doing everywhere; for every man has his own part to look after, which is as much as he can do, without minding what other people are about. Then, madam, there is such drumming and trumpeting, firing and smoking, fighting and rattling everywhere; and such an uproar of courage and slaughter in every man's mind; such a delightful confusion altogether that you can no more give an account of it that you can of the stars in the sky.

Another professionally polished playwright was Arthur Murphy (1727–1805), a man of letters, whose comedies and farces maintained a spanking pace. Hugh Kelly (1739–77), on the other hand, wallowed in sentiment; as a result he had a great contemporary success with his comedy *A School for Wives* (1774). Work by both playwrights is now coming into print again. Sentimentality, of course, had appeared elsewhere: it was a fashionable European cult that occasionally produced some fine literature. Ireland contributed its full share with Henry Brooke's (1703–83) novel *The Fool of Quality* (1766), or indeed rather more than its share if we consider the writings of Laurence Sterne (1713–68). His stream of consciousness was no doubt set flowing when, as a child in Clonmel, he fell into a mill race when the mill was working, and survived this early experience of turning on the wheel of fortune. He emerged safely from it, to become later the first modern novelist, abandoning plot, establishing experiment and innovation, finding it very hard in writing *Tristram Shandy* (1759–67) to mutilate everything in it 'down to the prudish humour of every particular'. Sterne explored characters in the privacy of their own associations of ideas, their subconsciousness exposed to his reflective reactions every bit as much as his own virtually instantaneously instinctive responses to emotional stimuli. Sterne is indeed modern in his attitude to identity:

My good friend, quoth I — as sure as I am I — and you are you — And who are you? said he — Don't puzzle me; said I

And in *A Sentimental Journey through France and Italy* (1768) he gets us to share his capacity for sentimentality *and* to appreciate the emotions of others. Sterne is never dull, his sense of humour includes self-mockery and an utterly modern capacity for stretching out his hand — and then leaving things in the air. It is done with a full realisation of the comedy of the absurd.

To return to Sterne's contemporaries, however, rather than compare him to our own, to consider the theatre proper of the eighteenth century, suggests that we should remember that Isaac Bickerstaffe (?1733–1808/12) was a pioneer in making comic opera popular in England, his *Love in a Village* (1761) being very successful indeed. And John O'Keefe (1747–1833) was another most successful author of operas, among them *The Son-in-Law* (1783), *The Wicklow Gold Mines, or, The Lady of the Hill* (1796) with its Irish setting, and *Wild Oats* (1792) which was revived by the Royal Shakespeare Company (in 1976).

To mention Hugh Kelly and his sentimental comedies is to think at once of how much Goldsmith disliked sentimental comedy, writing an essay against it, describing it as a bastard form of tragedy, and showing in his own two comedies *The Good Natur'd Man* (1768) and *She Stoops to Conquer* (1773) what he thought comedy ought to be. His comic sense is Elizabethan in its blend of irony, anticlimax, farce and absurdity; no wonder *She Stoops to Conquer* is still staged to the continuing delight of audiences. When Yeats wrote of Goldsmith sipping at the honey-pot of his mind he was probably referring not to Will Honeywood, the hero of *The Good Natur'd Man*, a character very like Goldsmith himself in his universal (and completely impractical) benevolence, but to *The Bee*, that civilised and elegant series of essays so typical — in their ease, their tolerance, their lighthearted irony and their balanced wisdom — of the best of the eighteenth century's civilised good taste. But it is perhaps surprising that Yeats did not include Sheridan with his other four Irish writers. The Sheridans are part and parcel of Irish literary life.

Richard Brinsley Sheridan's grandfather was Swift's witty and feckless schoolmaster friend; his father Thomas, apart from books on the English language, wrote tragedies and a farce with a gullible Irish hero suitably named Captain O'Blunder (1754); his mother, Frances, wrote two successful comedies, *The Discovery* (1763) being most effective. Richard Brinsley himself is now known mainly for his two polished and popular comedies *The Rivals* (1775) and *The School for Scandal* (1777). Their classical contrasts between appearance and reality, their wit and rich characterisation, their intrigue, their elegance and wit, and their dramatic skill so brilliantly displayed in suspense and unexpected reversals, still delight audiences in our day. But Sheridan was also a fine orator who was persuaded by his countryman Edmund Burke to speak against Warren Hastings in marathon performances — his first speech lasting five and a half hours and holding his audience enthralled. But then Sheridan, for all his being an MP and holding office, was a performer, an actor as well as a theatre owner and manager, and so he was a successful orator.

With the oratory of Henry Grattan (1746–1820), however outstanding it was in the Dublin of his day, then a city of orators — we are coming to the end of an era, to the last years of the rationalising eighteenth century. Burke foresaw the coming dangers of the French Revolution but he was not heeded: more quoted than read now, he gave wise advice then to English politicians, realising the likelihood of French influence igniting an outburst of revolution in Ireland. He argued eloquently that the English government should trust the Catholic Irish and emancipate them. But then came the Revolution of 1798 and after it the Act of Union, passed in 1800, which eliminated the Parliament in Dublin, and for a time had a devastating effect on Irish culture.

It is time to take stock of eighteenth century Irish writing. Some lesser known dramatists have been mentioned deliberately, though they are seldom discussed by critics. The great thesis machine has not yet ingested them: it is still busily digesting Joyce and Yeats, nibbling cautiously at the poets Austin Clarke and Patrick Kavanagh, and beginning to carve up Frank O'Connor, Liam O'Flaherty and Brendan Behan. Beckett is almost within sight; the thesis machine is insatiable, and will now swallow major authors alive, alive oh. But the dead minor authors of the eighteenth century, as their predecessors and indeed their successors too, are often not in print; few libraries harbour them, and yet they are rewarding to read: minor authors may be an acquired taste, but for a researcher they are required reading; and they often yield surprisingly interesting results. They were read by their contemporaries; they may not have risen above the fashions of their times but they often allow us insights into intellectual attitudes, and above all they return us admiringly to that inovative creative genius, which is the majesty and the might of major authors, for the basis of literary criticism depends upon comparison, upon our ability to recognise the differences, the complex range of writing contained within a literature.

Yeats's picture of the Irish eighteenth century is like some wall of ashlar masonry, with only four boulders surviving. But the pattern is more complex: there are authors of all sizes in it, medium and small as well as the four great ones, and a better image might be of a dry stone wall, such as we find so frequently in the west of Ireland, an artifact attractive in its variety of achievement.

How much more complex is the pattern in the nineteenth and twentieth centuries. To begin with, fiction must be added, and here we can see that innovation has been a dominant strain. Maria Edgeworth began it in 1800 by inventing the regional novel with her *Castle Rackrent*, telling the story of the rise and fall of four generations of the feckless, drinking, gambling Rackrent family through the words of a servant, Thady Quinn, who uses the lively English spoken by the Irish peasantry at that time. Maria Edgeworth's other Irish tales, *Ennui* (1809), *The Absentee* (1812) and *Ormond* (1817), fit her Irish material into the accepted pattern of the English novel and we can see the same method at work towards the end of the century in that superb novel by Somerville and Ross, *The Real Charlotte* (1894), full of observation of the nuances of Irish snobbery as well as a portrait of Charlotte Mullen's ruthless ambition destroying all her hopes. It is a strain that continues to the present day in, say, Michael Farrell's almost great novel *Thy Tears May Cease* (1963) or in the novels of Jennifer Johnston. They explore what have now become traditional themes: of the landlords in their big houses and their relationships with the country people who surround them.

Another kind of fictional experimentation based upon the antiquarian movement's investigation of Ireland's past history and culture was heralded by Lady Morgan's wildly romantic novel *The Wild Irish Girl* (1806), where the harp-playing heroine Glorvina instructs her English suitor about Ireland's traditions, her father being an old Irish chieftain living in a ruined castle, a symbol of the former grandeur of the Gaelic civilsation. Lady Morgan was followed by Charles Robert Maturin, an eccentric Irish clergyman of Huguenot extraction, who wrote the first account of an undergraduate's love affair in *Women*, or *Pour et Contre* (1818) — of which there are only about half a dozen copies in the world — and then went on to create the supreme achievement of that absurd genre the Gothic horror story in *Melmoth the Wanderer* (1820) — a genre to be developed further in the century.⁵ But Tom Moore's *Memoirs of Captain Rock* (1824) — a surprisingly unread novel — was nearer to the harsh realities of Irish life.

Maturin was often melodramatic, and so were the very different novelists who began to portray peasant life with disturbing realism. They included the Banim brothers, from Kilkenny, and William Carleton, a bilingual author from the northern county of Tyrone. In his *Traits and Stories of the Irish Peasantry* (1st series 1830; 2nd series 1833) Carleton conveys the pulsing vitality of an overcrowded and impoverished countryside that over-flowed into the violence of faction fights, that burgeoned in weddings and wakes, funerals and fairy tales. He was capturing the exuberance and energy of life in Ireland before the devastating famine of the mid-nineteenth century reduced the population by starvation, disease and emigration from over 8,000,000 in 1845 to 6,500,000 in 1851, and to 5,500,000 in 1871.⁶ Carleton's *The Black Prophet* (1847) and later Liam O'Flaherty's *Famine* (1937) treat the tragedy hauntingly; it is given a no less grim historical documentation in Cecil Woodham Smith's magnificent and moving book *The Great Hunger. Ireland 1845–9* (1962).

Comic energy, however, pulsated through the pages of Charles Lever's early novels *The Confessions of Harry Lorrequer* (1839) and *Charles O'Malley The Irish Dragoon* (1841), portraying the rollicking life of Irish students and soldiers. He has subsequently been dismissed by influential Irish critics⁷ as a mere entertainer of the English, a portrayer of the stage Irishman.⁸ Such critics have obviously not read Lever's middle and later novels with their sombre indictment of the ruling Anglo-Irish establishment,⁹ a dark portrayal of the future, matched by Emily Lawless's harsh picture of peasant life in County Clare, *Hurrish* (1886).

While the novelists portrayed Ireland from the viewpoints of gentry, middle class intellectuals, and peasantry, nineteenth century poetry was not at first outstanding. The landmarks are 1807, when Moore's *Irish Melodies* created a vast new audience in England and later in America for Irish subject matter, and 1888, when William Allingham's *Poetical Works* were published. Moore was helped by his friend Edward Hudson who had collected old Irish airs; both Moore and he had copies of the airs that Edward Bunting had set down at the famous festival of Irish harpers held in 1792 in Belfast, and Moore was writing in the wake of Edward Bunting's *General Collection of Ancient Irish Music* (1796). Bunting was yet another who was actively engaged in preserving knowledge of the Irish past; there was also an increasing number of translators of Irish poetry, notably Charlotte Brooke (daughter of Henry Brooke the novelist) who had published her pioneering *Reliques of Irish Poetry* in 1789.

Another effective translator was the Cork poet Jeremiah Joseph Callanan who wrote a long poem in Spenserian stanzas *The Outlaw of the Glen* in 1803; his *Collected Poems* (1861) show his innovations as a translator — he is best known for 'The Outlaw of Loch Lene', originally probably a folk poem:

> Oh, many a day have I made good ale in the glen
> That came not of stream, or malt, like the brewing of man;
> My bed was the ground; my roof the greenwood above
> And the wealth that I sought — one far kind glance from my love.

There were many Irish poets writing in English; their work has been represented in various anthologies, and some of them are worth more attention, for their work contains many good poems which have slipped through the inevitably coarse mesh of the anthologists' nets. These poets fall into three categories: those who are minor poets primarily influenced by the English romantics in their treatment of their material (not all of it Irish in subject); among them are Edward Lysaght (?1761–1810/11), James Orr (1770–1816), Sir Aubrey De Vere (1788–1846), Charles Wolfe (1791–1823), George Darley (1795–1846), Aubrey De Vere (1824–1902) — a far better poet than his father Sir Aubrey — Thomas Caulfield Irwin (1823–92), and John Francis O'Donnell (1837–74).

Then there are poets who were influenced in some of their work by Gaelic poetry. Among them are George Ogle (1739–1814), John Philpot Curran (1750–1817), a master of internal rhyming and assonance, and Thomas Furlong (1794–1827). But more impressive than these poets were James Clarence Mangan who captured, like Moore, the dragging cadences of Irish poetry in such poems as 'O'Hussey's Ode to the Maguire' or his famous 'Dark Rosaleen', and Sir Samuel Ferguson whose severely masculine verse was close to the tough, direct nature of his Irish originals and whose own original poetry is notable for lively experimentation.

The third category includes the idiosyncratic and entertaining poets Richard Milliken (1767–1815) and Francis Sylvester Mahoney (1804–66) who wrote as Father Prout. They parodied the style of Irish hedge-schoolmasters, they included fine displays of inconsequence and had a sharp sense of burlesque. They enjoyed the mock naive (particularly in their rhyming) which they employed in a peculiarly ironic way favoured by Irish intellectuals from Swift to Flann O'Brien. Here, for instance, is the last stanza of Milliken's 'The Groves of Blarney'

>There's statues gracing
>This noble place in —
>All heathen gods
>   And nymphs so fair;
>Bold Neptune; Plutarch,
>And Nicodemus,
>All standing naked
>   In the open air!
>So now to finish
>This brave narration
>Which my poor genii
>   Could not entwine;
>But were I Homer,
>Or Nebuchadnezzar,
>'Tis in every feature.
>   I would make it shine.

To this Mahoney added another final stanza:

>There is a stone there
>That whoever kisses
>Oh! he never misses
>   To grow eloquent;
>'Tis he may clamber
>To a lady's chamber
>Or become a member
>   Of parliament.
>A clever spouter
>He'll soon turn out, or
>An out-and-outer
>   To be let alone.
>Don't hope to hinder him,
>Or to bewilder him,
>Sure he's a pilgrim
>   From the Blarney Stone!

His own poem 'The Attractions of a Fashionable Irish Watering-place' is characteristic of the enjoyment he and Milliken got in parodying the absurdities of some itinerant Irish poets.

> The town of Passage
> Is both large and spacious
> and situated
>   Upon the say.
> 'Tis nate and dacent
> And quite adjacent
> To come from Cork
>   On a summer's day.
> There you may slip in
> To take a dipping
> Fornent the shipping
>   That at anchor ride,
> Or in a wherry
> Come o'er the ferry
> To Carrigaloe
>   On the other side...

William Allingham (1824–89) was mainly known for his anthology pieces such as 'The Faeries':

> Up the airy mountain
> Down the rushy glen
> We daren't go a-hunting
> For fear of little men;
> Wee folk, good folk
> Trooping all together;
> Green jacket, red cap
> And white owl's feather.

or the simple, less anthologised, yet most intense and pleasing 'Four Ducks on a Pond':

> Four ducks on a pond,
> A grass-bank beyond
> A blue sky of spring
> White clouds on the wing;
> What a little thing
> To remember for years —
> To remember with tears

Allingham transmitted his love of place in 'The Winding Banks of Erne: or, the Emigrant's adieu to Ballyshannon', naming local places with delight. As represented in earlier anthologies he seemed a quintessentially Victorian poet. Now, however, he is beginning to be greatly respected for the realism he put into the 2,300 heroic couplets of his *Laurence Bloomfield in Ireland* (1864), a devastating account of what might be called agrarian unrest — a murdered land agent, bailiffs, evictions, and the crushing poverty of much of the western countryside. He is most reminiscent of Crabbe, the English poet, who also drew his countryside in an unfashionable poetic mode but was equally a questioner of his age's treatment of the poor.

Allingham remains primarily a regional poet; he seemed to Yeats to have expressed a west of Ireland feeling. His *Collected Poems* (1888) marks the end of an era. Change was coming, and in all literary genres.

For the most developed and exciting experiment and innovation we come to an author who spanned nineteenth and twentieth centuries, George Moore. 'Zola's ricochet', he brought naturalism into English fiction with *Esther Waters* (1894), then returned to Ireland to write the stories of *The Untilled Field* (1903) before developing the melodic line in *The Lake* (1905) and subsequently creating his superbly mocking picture of Dublin in *Hail and Farewell* (1911, 1912, and 1914). Ever an experimenter, he moved on to the beauty of *Héloïse and Abelard* (1921) and the original thought and reflection of *The Brook Kerith* (1916). Moore's path was parallel to that of Joyce, the supreme fictional innovator.

Both men moved from realism — Moore's stories in *The Untilled Field* (1903) and Joyce's in *Dubliners* (1914) — to an impressionistic, often poetic prose which explored the subconscious — *The Lake* (1905) and *A Portrait of the Artist as a Young Man* (1916) — and from it to their very different Dublins — *Hail and Farewell* (1911, 1912 and 1914) and *Ulysses* (1922) — and then to the worlds of reverie and dream — *The Brook Kerith* (1916) and *Finnegans Wake* (1939).

Joyce is a completely twentieth-century author, though he bears the stigmata of the Irish Victorian upbringing from which he fled. His character Stephen Dedalus leaves Ireland 'to encounter for the millionth time the reality of experience and to forge in the smithy of my soul the uncreated conscience of my race'. In doing this he was, of course, following many another writer who found Ireland too small. George Bernard Shaw put it clearly:

> Every Irishman who felt that his business in life was on the higher planes of the cultural professions felt that he must have a metropolitan domicile and an international culture: that is, he felt that his first business was to get out of Ireland.[10]

Getting out of Ireland was for Shaw, as for so many other writers, an artistic necessity: a need to disengage in order to be cosmopolitan, a thing most of the dramatists had done, or to see their Ireland more clearly, as Joyce did. There was another factor, too: the need to earn a living, to find a larger audience. For many Irish writers there was another spur: they were poor relations. Goldsmith is a case in point. His father out of pride gave away his land and tithes in an attempt to match the marriage portion of one of his daughters to the wealth of her young husband — a generous gesture but one which impoverished the family and made life hard for young Oliver when he became an undergraduate at Trinity College, Dublin. Shaw put it well:

> I was a downstart and the son of a downstart... I sing my own class: the Shabby Genteel, the Poor Relations, the Gentlemen who are no Gentlemen...[11]

The problem of poverty was compounded by another problem. Shaw continued:

Our ridiculous poverty was too common in our class and not conspicuous enough in a poor country to account wholly for our social detachment from my father's family... Unfortunately or fortunately (it all depends how you look at it), my father had a habit which eventually closed all doors to him... If you asked him to a dinner or a party, he was not always quite sober when he arrived; and he was invariably scandalously drunk when he left.... We were finally dropped socially.[12]

We find the same situation in Joyce's family; the Joyces, too, were downstarts, and Joyce's father, like Shaw's, drank excessively. And though he did not drink, Yeats's father John Butler Yeats, the artist, did not support his family adequately, sending them frequently to stay in Sligo with his wife's relations because he had no funds. He held that a gentleman should not be concerned with getting on in the world. The importance given to the word 'gentleman' in Ireland is very significant as it indicated a social standing, however perilously the standing might be poised on the brink of poverty.

Between Shaw, born in 1856, and Joyce, born in 1882, came Yeats, born in 1865. When Yeats and Joyce met for the first time in Dublin in 1902 Joyce, then twenty, reputedly told Yeats, then thirty-seven, that he was too old for Joyce to help him. He objected to everything Yeats was doing, asked him why he had concerned himself with politics, with folklore, with the historical setting of events and so on.[13] We can interpret a passage in *A Portrait of the Artist as a Young Man* as showing Stephen Dedalus fearing the pull of the Irish revival on him. The entry in his diary for April 14 [which probably alludes to John Millington Synge] reads:

> John Alphonsus Mulrennan has just returned from the west of Ireland. European and Asiatic papers please copy. He told us he met an old man there in a mountain cabin. Old man had red eyes and short pipe. Old man spoke Irish. Mulrennan spoke Irish. Then old man and Mulrennan spoke English. Mulrennan spoke to him about universe and stars. Old man sat, listened, smoked, spat. Then said:
>
> — Ah there must be terrible creatures at the latter end of the world.
>
> I fear him. I fear his redrimmed horny eyes. It is with him I must struggle all through this night till day come, till he or I lie dead, gripping him by the sinewy throat till . . . Till what? Till he yield to me? No I mean no harm.[14]

Yeats had begun to alter the whole Irish literary pattern, the possibilities for Irish writers. Here is where a good library can help, for there are so many threads to be followed — perhaps one of the first is the effect of journals such as *The Nation* which Thomas Davis began in 1842, and which had a profound effect upon Irish readers, arousing in them feelings of patriotic pride in their non-British heritage. John Mitchel, whose *Jail Journal* (1854) is a classic account of nineteenth century penal punishment, established the more nationalist and influential *United Irishman* in 1848. Serious discussion of Ireland's past, present and future, at a generally more intellectual level, had been pursued in the *Dublin University Magazine*, a journal founded earlier in

1833 by Isaac Butt and five others.[15] We need further studies of the effects of these and many other journals as well as an examination of the conditions and the effects of Irish publishing.[16]

Despite the fiasco of the Fenian rising of 1867 the spirit of the Fenians lived on strongly in the United States among the Irish American community, while in Ireland itself resistance to English rule found expression in Parnell's leadership of the Irish party in the House of Commons. This ended with the O'Shea divorce case in which he was cited as co-respondent in 1890 and his death the following year. There was a continuing and increasing interest in the cultural as well as the political and economic differences between Ireland and England. Several authors had been trying to re-energise Irish mythology — Sir Samuel Ferguson and Standish O'Grady in particular — while others were concerned to preserve a Gaelic identity. Douglas Hyde, poet and translator, founded the Gaelic League in 1893 to foster the Irish language and culture, as he put it, to de-Anglicise Ireland. (A somewhat parallel movement had developed earlier in the rurally based Gaelic Athletic Association founded in 1884 to promote Irish games, particularly hurling.) Yeats thought he could himself blend pagan and Christian elements in poetry which would escape the cliches of past patriotic rhetoric. After Parnell's death he spent a great deal of energy organising literary societies and creating a movement which would make Ireland aware of its impressive heritage.

Why the appearance of Allingham's *Poetical Works* in 1888 can be regarded as the end of a phase is that the following year Yeats's *The Wanderings of Oisin* marked a new development, the emergence of Irish mythological material presented in an elegant and effective way. In interpreting the early legends and tales, Yeats brought in a sensuous quality the older poet Sir Samuel Ferguson had lacked. He had found a way past the historical and imperialist English mythology that he had met in his English school: the victory of Agincourt left him unmoved. And equally the defeat of Aughrim, part of Irish historical and nationalist mythology, had not appealed to him. At the age of twenty-three he was a romantic, and he had found a way of creating his own world. Now he could be free of his poetic elders, escape the example of Tennyson's Arthuriad, of Arnold's classicism, of Browning's Renaissance. What need of them; he would himself create a Celtic Renaissance[17] in Ireland. He came to the conclusion, however, that the Irish were not a nation of readers. They were, he said, 'a people who sing songs and make speeches and like to listen'. And that was why, he added, he had decided 'to devote his energies to the theatre'.[18]

His theatre was to be — unlike the theatres in England and America which had welcomed Dion Boucicault's meldodramas — such as *The Colleen Bawn, or The Brides of Garryowen* (1860), *Arrah-na-Pogue; or the Wicklow Wedding* (1865) and *The Shaughraun* (1881) — or those which later enjoyed Wilde and Shaw triumphantly reviving the comedy of manners, sophisticating or, in Shaw's case, socialising, its scepticism, teasing the English establishment (which, to its credit, loved this). Wilde and Shaw had been successfully inverting the conventions and pushing the paradox further than it would normally proceed. No, Yeats wanted none of this; he wanted an Irish theatre, with Irish actors and actresses playing Irish plays in Ireland. With the help of Lady Gregory — and for a time Edward Martyn, another neighbouring Galway landowner, and George Moore, himself a Mayo landlord — he managed to create the Abbey to which Synge's plays gave the cachet of controversy.

The Abbey audiences were not wildly enthusiastic about Yeats's heroic plays — though his patriotic play *Cathleen ni Houlihan*, produced in 1902, had a stirring effect that worried him in old age in 1938:

> Did that play of mine send out
> Certain men the English shot[19]

His own battling was first for Synge's plays and later for Sean O'Casey's, for both authors aroused the ire of nationalists, who disregarded their artistic brilliance, regarding them as denigrators of the popular, patriotic image of Ireland.

This kind of battle continued throughout the nineteen twenties, 'thirties and 'forties. The establishment of the new Irish state led to censorious attitudes towards art in general. Indeed the negative decisions of the newly established official Censorship Boards were often absurd. And so many of the young revolutionaries found the Ireland they had fought to bring into being was restrictive and puritanical. Frank O'Connor, Liam O'Flaherty and Sean O'Faolain found their works banned in their own country and so did younger writers such as Edna O'Brien. One of the reasons why Yeats was so involved in establishing the Irish Academy of Letters in 1932 was that such a body might be most vigorous, capable of defending the interests of authors, 'negotiating with Government, and I hope capable of preventing the worst forms of censorship'.[20] In discussing the Academy[21] he explained the troubles as caused by Irish criticism being political rather than literary. The Academy, he said, would attempt to criticise from a literary point of view:

> It will 'crown' books. It will try to fight for a modification of the censorship laws. In Ireland we have had to fight the mob. Some time ago there was a proposal to tax books. Probably it will arise again. We shall fight that.[22]

He extracted some general ideas from the subject, relating the whole grand and better phase of Irish life — like that of Sean O'Casey — to the spirit of self-criticism which arose after the collapse of the Parnell movement. He thought Ireland's tragic situation had helped to produce good drama. He cited Joyce as a prime example of the Irish spirit of remorseless criticism, saying 'his vitality grew out of the bitterest period' and adding that he did not see the bitterness disappearing 'for it was an attempt to reduce uselessness in the nation. So it should be remorseless.'

We are coming to the close of a century full of Irish literary achievement. After the creativity of Yeats in poetry; of Joyce in the novel; of Shaw, Synge and O'Casey in drama; of Hyde and Lady Gregory in translation, what happened? We need to have a panoramic vista of the full shelves of a unique library to realise the impact of the Irish literary Renaissance on succeeding generations. It is almost inevitable that aspects of the literary movement should now be beginning to be denigrated[23] — George Moore sent it up with guesto, malice and barbed wit in *Hail and Farewell* — for criticism swings back and forth like a pendulum over the years. Nonetheless the Revival compensated for the small readership offered by a small country — given, as Yeats remarked, to talk and singing — and without a strong publishing industry, by creating a readership in Britain, Europe and, especially, North America.

Things have certainly changed as a result of this impact of the Literary Renaissance. More people publish books in Ireland, and very successfully, too, in many cases. They are extremely adept, for instance, at selling foreign rights to them — as anyone who has visited the great Book Fair at Frankfurt knows. And more people read books by Irish authors, now issued by publishers in Ireland, Britain or America, singly or, increasingly, in collaboration. The Irish Literary Renaissance gave Irish writing international status, and the Irish government has recognised the importance of literature by giving writers living in Ireland a unique status, of not paying income tax on their artistic earnings.

There is no pressing need, now, for Irish writers to leave Ireland in search of an audience — or indeed to leave it in the spirit of Shaw or Joyce or Beckett. They do not necessarily need to find their inspiration in Ireland. Look at contemporary writers such as Iris Murdoch or William Trevor,[24] Francis Stuart or Derek Mahon. They choose to write on Irish subjects, or not, as they wish, following in the traditions of Elizabeth Bowen, Joyce Cary, C. S. Lewis, or Louis MacNeice. But they are no less Irish writers for this spread of interest. There remain authors who continue to find their material mainly in Ireland, Mary Lavin, for instance, or Brian Moore, who carries Ireland with him, to Canada, to the United States.[25] John Banville, one of the most impressive younger novelists, reacts against what he thinks are the obsessions of Irish fiction: politics, religion and repressed sexuality.[26] So he writes on the relationships between science and art.[27]

Many Irish authors have found the short story a congenial genre, particularly in the twentieth century. As Anthony Burgess remarks, in his Preface to *Modern Irish Short Stories* (1980), Irish writers excel in brief forms, lyrical or dramatic. He emphasises their achievement in brief narrative, calling this the form in which they excel. He points out that these short story writers have in common an awareness of verbal tradition. They set up an atmosphere in a few words, he says, attributing this to 'the practical element in the Irish'.

Poetry after Yeats seemed, for a time, to be dominated by Austin Clarke who had begun as a 'celtic' poet but toughened into a satirist, and by Patrick Kavanagh whose later poems had a philosophical acceptance of life. There are many poets writing today who are impressive by any standards, notably Seamus Heaney, a most gifted thinker and poetic technician, and there are other Northern poets as well, such as John Montague, Michael Longley and James Simmons. The roll call of all the poets writing in Ireland is long, and I will merely mention Thomas Kinsella, Brendan Kennelly and Richard Murphy. You will yourselves automatically add names, add ideas to the list of what is, intrinsically, Irish poetry and in so doing remind yourselves of the unbounded claims of that literature.

And yet they share an inheritance, whether they come from north and south : these writers have a homogeneity which needs to be appreciated and understood. Like Brian Friel or Hugh Leonard in the theatre, they share a background, and one that their fellow Irishmen, born into an oral tradition, fully apprehend. Their words can wing the world : in an age of instant communication, television or jet bring these words to ever-growing audiences. It is ultimately, however, in a great specialised research library, such as this rapidly developing and most welcome Princess Grace Irish Library, that men and women will be able to ponder their words in print and link them to the great and varied tradition out of which they come and so help us all to enjoy them the more.

Notes

1. And with each other's writings. Here, for example, is a relationship not commented on before to which Mr Warwick Gould has recently drawn my attention. In Chapter 22 of George Moore's *Evelyn Innes* (1898) Ulick Dean, who is modelled on Yeats, kissed Evelyn Innes on the cheek: 'but at the instant of the touching of his lips, she threw her arms about his neck, and drew him down as mermaid draws her mortal lover into the depths, and in a wondering world of miraculous happiness he surrendered himself' (p. 294). Here is an image used by Yeats in his poem 'The Mermaid', included in the series 'A Man Young and Old', written in 1926 and 1927.

    > A mermaid found a swimming lad,
    > Picked him for her own,
    > Pressed her body to his body,
    > Laughed; and plunging down
    > Forgot in cruel happiness
    > That even lovers drown.
    > *Collected Poems* (1950) p. 250

    Another source could be Lady Gregory's *Visions and Beliefs in the West of Ireland* (1920): 'And there was a boy saw a mermaid down by Spidal [Co. Galway] not long ago, but he saw her before she saw him, so she did him no harm. But if she'd seen him first, she'd have brought him away and drowned him' (Coole Edition, 1970, p. 19). Yeats's poem is about his affair with Mrs Shakespear. For her part in bringing it about, see W. B. Yeats, *Memoirs*, ed. Denis Donoghue (1972), pp. 85–89, and A. Norman Jeffares, *W. B. Yeats: Man and Poet* (1962), pp. 100–103. See also *The Collected Letters of W. B. Yeats Volume I, 1865–1895*, ed. John Kelly (1986), pp. 511–12; letters from George Moore to Yeats of 3 and 28 October and 24 November 1898. The letter of 28 October states that Chapter 22 of *Evelyn Innes* is entirely rewritten 'and in the intention of converting an episode into a symbol'. The letters are included in *Letters to W. B. Yeats*, edited by Richard J. Finneran, George Mills Harper and William M. Murphy (1977), pp. 41, 42, 44 and 45.

2. Swift, incidentally, may not have known Irish but that did not stop him translating an Irish poem 'O'Rourke's Feast' by an Irish poet, Hugh MacGowran, whom he did know. This is one of the earliest translations of Irish poetry we have.

3. His views resemble those of William Molyneux (1656–98), a Dublin M.P. who had published *The Case of Ireland being bound by Acts of Parliament in England, Stated*, in 1698. In this he had argued that Ireland owed allegiance to the King but not to the Westminster Parliament: 'Have not Multitudes of Acts of Parliament both in England and Ireland declared Ireland a compleat Kingdom Is not Ireland stiled in them all, the Kingdom or Realm of Ireland? Do these Names agree to a Colony? Have we not a Parliament and Courts of Judicature? Do these things agree with a Colony?'

4 W. B. Yeats, *Wheels and Butterflies*, (1934), p. 7.
5 Sheridan Le Fanu's novels explore the supernatural future later in the century, and his *Carmilla* in its turn probably inspired Bram Stoker's *Dracula* (1897). And Oscar Wilde's *The Picture of Dorian Gray* (1891) can perhaps be considered a continuation of this strain.
6 J. C. Beckett, *A Short History of Ireland* (1952), pp. 156–57. He remarks: 'The famine began with a partial failure of the potato crop in the autumn of 1845, it reached its height during 1846 and 1847, by 1848 the wrost was over. During these four years Ireland had lost, by death and emigration, over 1,000,000 of her people; in 1847 alone it is reckoned that almost 250,000 died of starvation or fever and over 200,000 fled to America.'
7 Notably Yeats and Lady Gregory.
8 The stage Irishman's first appearance seems to have occurred as far back as 1689 when James Farewell satirised the exuberance of Irish mythological material in *The Irish Hudibras*, or *Fingallian Prince*.
9 See, for example, *Roland Cashel* (1848) and *Con Cregan* (1849) and his later novels, *Barrington* (1862), *Sir Brook Fossbrooke* (1865) and *Lord Kilgobbin* (1872).
10 In 'Preface: Fragments of an Autobiography', included in George Bernard Shaw, *The Master with Ireland* (1962), p. 10.
11 Shaw, *The Matter with Ireland*, p. 1.
12 *Ibid.*, pp. 4–5.
13 See Richard Ellmann, *James Joyce*, new and revised ed., 1982, pp. 100–104.
14 James Joyce, *A Portrait of the Artist as a Young Man* (1916).
15 It was at one time owned by Sheridan Le Fanu, and Charles Lever edited it from 1842–45.
16 And we badly need further collections of ballads to enable us to understand the oral traditions of the nineteenth and twentieth centuries.
17 Celticism was, of course, in the air. There was a European interest in the subject. In France Ernest Renan was writing about the Celtic poetry of his native Brittany, Marie Henri Arbois de Jubainville had founded the *Revue Celtique* and written several influential books on Celtic Literature and Irish mythology. In Germany Rudolf Thurneysen, Heinrich Zimmer, Ernest Windisch and especially Kuno Meyer, famous for his translations of Irish poetry, were actively pursuing their scholarship in Irish studies. In England Matthew Arnold was praising the energies of the Celtic people in his *On the Study of Celtic Literature* (1867).
18 'Many years ago'; he was talking in an interview which appeared under the heading 'Irish Poet Here, Talks on Affairs of His Nation', published in the *Detroit News*, on 12 November 1932, p. 19.
19 W. B. Yeats, 'The Man and the Echo', *Collected Poems* (1950), p. 393.
20 W. B. Yeats, *Letters*, ed. A. Wade (1954), p. 801.
21 With an American reporter; see 'Yeats Arrives on Europa for Play Opening', *New York Herald Tribune*, 7 October, 1932, p. 3.
22 He was correct in his prophecy. Purchase tax was imposed on books some years ago but, happily, lifted again.
23 See, for instance, Declan Kiberd, 'The Perils of Nostalgia: A critique of the Revival', in *Literature and the Changing Ireland*, ed. Peter Connolly, 1982, pp. 1–24.

24 In a recent BBC interview on 'Bookman' in March 1986, Trevor dealt amusingly with a tendency in Ireland to divide Irish authors into the categories of 'writers' or 'Irish writers' — the implication being that the second category is restricted by a regionalism of subject matter.
25 Particularly in his moving novel *Fergus* (1971) in which a novelist's father appears to him in California, to question his way of his life rather than assess his achievement.
26 See Eileen Battersby, 'John Banville', *Books & Bookmen*, 365, March 1986, pp. 20–21.
27 See his *Doctor Copernicus* (1976), *Kepler* (1981) and *The Newton Letter* (1985).

A Select List of Irish Authors

AE; see Russell, George W.
Alexander, Frances, 1818–95
Allen, Alfred, b. 1925
Allgood, Molly (Maire O'Neill), 1887–1952
Allgood, Sara, 1883–1950
Allingham, William, 1824–89
Alpha and Omega; see Gogarty, Oliver St John
An Pilibin (John Hacket Pollock), 1887–1964
Arnold, Bruce
Astbury, Joseph, 1638–1720
Auchmuty, James Johnson, 1909–81

Balfe, Michael William, 1808–70
Ball, John, 1818–89
Banim, John, 1798–1842
Banim, Michael, 1796–1874
Banville, John, b. 1945
Bardwell, Leland, b. 1928
Barlow, Jane, 1859–1876
Barrett, Eaton Stannard, 1786–1820
Barrington, George, 1755–?
Barrington, Sir Jonah, 1760–1834
Barrington, Margaret, ?b. 1895–?
Barry, Lo (Lod/Lodwick), b. 1591?
Barry, Michael
Barry, Sebastian
'Basil'; see King, Richard Ashe
Beaslai, Piaras, 1881–1965

Beckett, James Camlin, b. 1912
Beckett, Samuel, b. 1906
Bedell, William, 1571–1642
Behan, Brendan, 1923–64
Behan, Dominic, b. 1928
Bell, Sam Hanna, b. 1909
Bence-Jones, Mark, b. 1930
Bergin, Osborn Joseph, 1873–1950
Berkeley, George (Bishop of Cloyne), 1685–1753
Bermingham, Peter de, d. 1308
Best, Richard Irvine, 1872–1959
Bibby, Thomas, 1799–1863
Bickerstaffe, Isaac, ?1753–1808
Binchy, Daniel, A., b. 1900
Binchy, Maeve, b. 1940
Bird, W.; see Yeats, Jack B.
Birmingham, George A. (Rev. J. O. Hannay), 1865–1950
Blackwood, Caroline (Maureen), b. 1931
Blake, Nicholas; see Day-Lewis, Cecil
Blessington, Countess of (Marguerite Power), 1789–1849
Blinco, Anthony, b. 1934
Blythe, Ernest, 1899–1975
Bodkin, Thomas, 1887–1961
Boland, Eavan, b. 1945
Bolger, Dermot, b. 1959
Boucicault, Dion, 1822–99
Bourke/Burke, James, see de Burca, Seamus
Bourke, Patrick, 1882–1932

Bowen, Elizabeth, 1899–1973
Boyd, Ernest A., 1887–1946
Boyd, John, b. 1912
Boyd, Thomas, 1867–1927
Boylan, Clare, b. 1948
Boylan, Eugene, 1904–64
Boyle, John, 5th Earl of Orrery, 1707–62
Boyle, Patrick, b. 1905
Boyle, Robert, 1627–91
Boyle, Roger, 1621–79
Boyle, William, 1853–1922
Brady, George M., 1917–?
Brady, Nicholas, 1652–1715
Breatnach, Padraig A., b. 1947
Brennan, Eileen, b. 1912
Brennan, Robert, b. 1881
Brock, Lynn; see McAllister, Alister (and Wharton, Anthony P.)
Broderick, John, b. 1927
Bronte, Rev Patrick, 1777–1861
Brooke, Augustus Stopford, 1832–1916
Brooke, Charlotte, 1740–93
Brooke, Henry, 1703–83
Brophy, Robert; see Ray, R. J.
Brown, Christy, b. 1932
Brown, Frances, 1816–79
Browne, Monsignor Patrick, 1889–1960
Brown, Rev., Stephen James Meredith, 1881–1962
Brownlow, Timothy, b. 1941
Buchanan, George, b. 1904
Bullock, Shan, 1865–1935
Bunbury, Selina, 1802–82
Bunting, Edward, 1773–1843
Burca, Seamus de (James Bourke/Burke); see de Burca, Seamus
Burgh, Walter Hussey, 1742–83
Burke, Edmund, 1729–97

Burke, John, 1787–1848
Burke, Richard, fl. 1600
Burke, Thomas, ?1710–76
Bury, John Bagenal, 1861–1927
Butt, Isaac, 1813–79
Byrne, Laurence Patrick; see Malone, Andrew E., 1888–1939
Byrne, Donn (Bryan Oswald Donn Byrne), 1889–1928
Byrne, Seamus, 1904–68
Byrne, Miles, 1780–1862

Callanan, Jeremiah Joseph, 1795–1829
Campbell, Joseph, 1879–1944
Campbell, Michael, 1924–
Campbell, Patrick, 1913–1980
Campion, John (Thomas), 1814–?
Carbery, Ethna (Anna Isabel Johnston née MacManus), 1866–1902
Carew, Rivers, b. 1935
Carleton, William, 1794–1869
Carlin, Frances, 1881–1945
Carney, James, b. 1914
Carolan, Turlogh, 1670–1738
Carty, James, 1901–59
Carroll, Paul Vincent, 1900–68
Cary, (Arthur) Joyce (Lunel), 1888–1957
Casement, Sir Roger, 1864–1916
Casey, John Keegan, 1846–70
Casey, Juanita, b. 1925
Casey, Kevin, b. 1940
Casey, Philip, b. 1950
Casey, William Francis, 1884–1957
Centlivre, Susannah, 1667–1722
Chadwick, George, 1840–?
Childers, (Robert) Erskine, 1870–1922

Cheyney, Peter (Reginald Evelyn Peter Southouse-Cheney), 1896–1951
Clarke, Austin, 1896–1974
Clarke, Desmond, b. 1907
Clarke, Joseph, 1846–1925
Cleeve, Brian, b. 1921
Clifford, Sigerson, b. 1913
Coffey, Brian, b. 1905
Coffey, Charles, ?1700–45
Coffey, Tom, b. 1925
Coghill, Rhoda, b. 1903
Collis, John Stewart, 1900–84
Collis, Maurice, 1889–1973
Collis (William), Robert (Fitzgerald), 1900–75
Colum, Mary, 1884–1957
Colum, Padraic, 1881–1972
Comyn, Michael, 1688–1760
Concannon, Helena, 1878–1952
Congreve, William, 1670–1729
Connell, F. Norreys (Conal O'Riordan), 1874–1948
Connell, Vivian, b. 1903
Conner (Patrick) Rearden, b. 1907
Connolly, Cyril Vernon, 1903–74
Connolly, Father Peter
Connor, Elizabeth, ?fl. 1940
Conyers, Dorothea, b. 1871–?
Cope, Joan Penelope (Lady Grant), b. 1926
Corkery, Daniel, 1878–1964
Costello, Louisa Stuart, 1799–1870
Costello, Peter
Coulter, John, b. 1888
Cousins, James Henry (Sproul), 1873–1956
Coyne, Joseph Stirling, 1803–68
Craig, Maurice James, b. 1919
Crofts, Freeman Wills, 1879–1957

Croker, John Wilson, 1780–1857
Croker, Thomas Crofton, 1798–1854
Crone, Anne, 1915–72
Crone, John Smyth, 1858–1945
Cronin, Anthony, b. 1926
Cross, Eric, b. 1903
Cummins, Geraldine Dorothy, b. 1890
Cunningham, John, 1729–73
Curran, John Philpot, 1750–1817
Curtin, Jeremiah, 1838–1906
Curtis, Edmund, 1881–1943
Cusack, Margaret F., 1832–99
Cusack, Cyril

Daiken, Leslie, 1900–51
Danby, Frank; see Frankau, Julia
D'Alton, John, 1792–1814
D'Alton, Louis, 1900–51
Dalton, Maurice
Daly, Rev Dominic, 1595–1662
Daly, Ita, b. 1945
Daly, Leo, b. 1920
Darley, George, 1795–1846
Davis, Thomas Osborne, 1814–45
Davitt, Michael, 1846–1906
Dawe, Gerald, b. 1952
Day-Lewis, Cecil, 1904–72
Deane, John F. b. 1943
Deane, Seamus, b. 1940
de Blacam, Aodh, 1890–1951
de Burca, Seamus (James (Bourke/Burke), b. 1912
Deeley, Patrick
Deevy, Teresa, 1903–63
de Faoite, Seamus, 1915–80
Denham, Sir John, 1615–69
De Paor, Liam, b. 1926

De Paor (*née* MacDermott), Marie, b. 1925
Dermody, Thomas, 1775–1802
De Vere, Sir Aubrey, 1788–1846
De Vere, Aubrey, 1814–1902
Devlin, Denis, 1908–59
Digby, Kenelm Henry, 1800–80
Dillon, Eilis, b. 1920
Dillon, Myles, 1900–72
Dillon, Wentworth, 4th Earl of Roscommon, 1633–85
Dineen, Father Padraig, 1860–1934
Dobbs, Francis, 1750–1811
Dodds, E. R., 1893–
Doggett, Thomas, ?1660–1721
Donaghy, John Lyle, 1902–47
Donleavy, James Patrick, b. 1920
Donnelly, Charles, 1914–37
Donoghue, Denis, b. 1928
Dopping, Anthony, 1643–97
Dowden, Edward, 1843–1913
Doyle, Lynn (Leslie Alexander Montgomery), 1873–1961
Drennan, John Swanwick, 1809–93
Drennan, William, 1754–1820
Dufferin, Lady Helen Selina, 1807–67
Duffet, Thomas, *fl.* 1676
Duffy, Bernard, ?–1952
Duffy, Sir Charles Gavin, 1816–1903
Dunkin, Rev. William, b. 1707–?
Dunleavy, James Patrick, b. 1926
Dunne (Christopher) Lee, b. 1934
Dunne, Sean
Dunsany, Lord Edward Moreton Drax Plunkett, 1878–1957
Durcan, Paul, b. 1944

Edgeworth, Maria, 1767–1849
Edgeworth, Richard Lovell, 1744–1817
Edwards, Hilton, 1903–82
Egan, Desmond, b. 1936
Egan, Pierce, 1772–1840
Egan, Pierce, 1814–80
Egerton, George (Mary Chavelita Dunne), 1859–1945
Eglinton, John (W. K. Magee), 1868–1961
Ellis, Conleth, b. 1937
Ervine, St John (Greer), 1883–1971
Emmet, Robert, 1778–1803
Ennis, John, b. 1944
Ewart, Gavin

Falcon, Edmund, 1814–79
Faller, Kevin, b. 1920
Fallon, Gabriel, 1898–1980
Fallon, Padraic, 1905–74
Fallon, Peter, b. 1951
Farewell, James, *fl.* 1689
Farquhar, George, 1678–1707
Farrell, Bernard, b. 1939
Farrell, James G., b. 1935
Farrell, M. J. (Molly Keane), b. 1905
Farrell, Michael, 1899/1900–62
Farren, Robert (Roibeard O'Farachain), 1909–84
Farrington, Conor Anthony, b. 1928
Faulkner, George, 1966–1775
Fay, William George, 1872–1947
Ferguson, Sir Samuel, 1810–86
Ferriter, Pierce, d. 1653
Fiacc, Padraic (Patrick Joseph O'Connor), b. 1924
Figgis, Darrell, 1882–1925
Fitzgerald, Desmond
Fitzgerald, Edward, 1809–83
Fitzgerald, Nigel, b. 1906

Fitzgerald, Percy Hetherington, 1834–1925
Fitzgibbon (Robert Louis) Constantine, 1919–83
Fitzgibbon, Theodora, b. 1916
Fitzmaurice, George, 1878–1963
Fitzpatrick, William John, 1830–95
Flanagan, Tom
Flannery, Thomas, 1840–1916
Flecknoe, Richard, b. ?1600
Flower, Robin, 1881–1946
Flynn, Mannix, b. 1957
Foley, Michael, b. 1947
French (William) Percy, 1854–1920
Francis, Sir Philip, 1708–73
Frankau, Julia (Frank Danby), 1864–1916
Friel, Brian, b. 1929
Froude, James Anthony, 1818–94
Furlong, Alice, b. 1875
Furlong, Thomas, 1794–1827

Gallagher, Frank, 1893–1962
Gallagher, Patrick (Paddy the Cope), 1873–1966
Gallivan, G. P., b. 1920
Galvin, Patrick, b. 1927
Gannor, Nicholas John, b. 1831
Gentleman, Frances, 1728–84
Geoghegan, Arthur, 1810–89
Gerald, Baron of Offaly, 1560–81
Gerald the Rhymer, 4th Earl of Desmond, d. 1398
Gibbings, Robert John, 1889–1958
Gibbon, Monk, b. 1896
Gilbert, Sir John, 1829–98
Gilbert, Lady; see Mulholland, Rosa
Gilbert, Stephen, b. 1912

Giolla, Caoimhghin, d. 1072
Godfrey, D(enis) R.
Godley, Alfred Denis, 1856–1925
Gogarty, Oliver St John (Alpha and Omega), 1878–1957
Goldsmith, Oliver, 1728–74
Gonne, Maud (Maud Gonne MacBride), 1866–1953
Gore-Booth, Eva, 1870–1926
Grattan, Henry, 1746–1820
Graves, Alfred Perceval, 1846–1931
Greacen, Robert, b. 1920
Green, Alice Stopford (née Kells), 1847–1929
Green, Frederick Laurence, 1902–53
Greacen, Robert, b. 1920
Gregory, Lady (Isabella) Augusta, 1852–1932
Griffin, Gerald, 1803–40
Griffith, Arthur, 1872–1922
Groves, Edward, c. 1775–?1850
Guinness, Bryan Walter, 2nd Baron Moyne, b. 1905
Gwynn, Stephen, 1864–1950

Hackett, Francis, 1883–1962
Hall, Mrs Anna Maria (née Fielding), 1800–81
Halloran, Laurence Hynes, 1766–1831
Halpine, Charles Graham, 1829–68
Hanaghan, Jonathan, 1887–1967
Hanley, Gerald
Hanley, James, b. 1901
Hannay, Rev. J. O.; see Birmingham, George A.
Hardiman, James, c. 1790–1855
Hardy, Elizabeth, 1704–1854
Harris, (Frank) James Thomas, 1855–1931

Hartnett, Michael, b. 1941
Hayes, Daniel, ?fl. 1730
Hayes, Richard James, 1902–76
Head, Richard, ?b. 1637–78
Healy, Gerard, 1918–63
Heaney, Seamus, b. 1939
Henn, Thomas Rice, 1901–74
Henry, James, 1798–1876
Hewitt, John, b. 1907
Hickey, William, 1749–1830
Higgins, Aidan, b. 1927
Higgins, F. R., 1896–1961
Hinkson, H. A., 1865–1919
Hinkson, Katherine; see Tynan, Katherine
Hinkson, Pamela, 1900–82
Hoey, Mrs Cashel (née Johnston), 1830–1908
Hogan, Desmond, b. 1951
Holloway, Joseph, 1861–1944
Hone, Joseph, b. 1937
Hone, Joseph Maunsell, 1882–1959
Hopper, Nora (Mrs Chesson), 1871–1906
Hoult, Norah, 1898–1984
Hudson, Edward
Hull, Eleanor, 1860–1935
Hutchinson, Pearse, b. 1927
Hyde, Douglas, 1860–1949
Hyde (Harford) Montgomery, b. 1907

Inglis, Brian, b. 1916
Ingram, John Kells, 1823–1907
Iremonger, Valentin, b. 1918
Irwin, Thomas Caulfield, 1823–92
Isdell, Sarah, ?b. 1780–?

Jackson, Kenneth, b. 1909
Jeffares, Alexander Norman (**Derry**), **b. 1920**

Jennet, Sean, b. 1910
Jofroi (of Waterford), d. 1300
Johnston, Anna Isobel; see Carbery, Ethna
Johnston, Charles
Johnston, Jennifer, b. 1930
Johnston (William) Denis, 1901–85
Johnstone, Charles, 1719–1800
Johnstone, Robert
Jones, Henry, 1721–70
Jordan, John, b. 1930
Jordan, Neil, b. 1951
Joyce, James, 1882–1941
Joyce, Patrick Weston, 1827–1914
Joyce, Robert Dwyer, 1830–63

Kavanagh, Michael, 1827–1900
Kavanagh, Patrick, 1905–67
Kavanagh, Peter
Kavanagh, Rose
Keane, John B., b. 1928
Keane, Molly; see Farrell, M. J.
Kearney, Michael
Kearney, Peadar, 1883–1942
Keating, Geoffrey, ?1570–?1650
Kell, Richard, b. 1907
Kelleher, Daniel Laurence, 1883–?
Kelly, Hugh, 1739–?
Kelly, James Plunkett; see Plunkett, James
Kelly, Maeve, b. 1930
Kennedy, Patrick, 1801–73
Kennelly, Brendan, b. 1936
Kenney, James, 1780–1849
Kiberd, Declan
Kickham, Charles Joseph, 1828–82
Kiely, Benedict, b. 1919
Kiely, Jerome, b. 1925
Kilroy, Thomas, b. 1934

King, Richard Ashe ('Basil'),
   1839–1932
King, William, 1670–1729
Kinsella, Thomas, b. 1928
Knowles, James Sheridan, 1784–
   1862

Lalor, Matthew, b. 1937
Lane, Temple (Mary Isabel
   Leslie), 1899–?
Lanyon, Helen, 1887–1935
Larminie, William, 1850–1900
Laverty, Maura, b. 1907
Lavin, Mary, b. 1912
Lawless, the Hon Emily, 1845–
   1913
Lawrence, W. J., 1862–1940
Leadbeater, Mary, 1758–1826
Lecky, William Edward
   Hartpole, 1838–1903
Ledwidge, Francis, 1887–1917
Ledrede, Richard de, c. 1316–60
Le Fanu (Joseph) Sheridan,
   1814–73
Leonard, Hugh (John Keyes
   Byrne), b. 1928
Leslie, Anita, b. 1914
Leslie, Sir Shane, 1885–1971
Letts, Winifred, b. 1882–?
Lever, Charles (James), 1806–72
Lewis, Clive Stapes, 1898–1963
Liddy, James, b. 1934
Little, Philip Frances, 1866–1926
Longford, Earl of; Pakenham,
   Edward Arthur Henry,
   1902–61
Longford, Lady; Christine Patti
   (née Trew), b. 1900
Longley, Michael, b. 1934
Lover, Samuel, 1797–1868
Luce, Arthur Aston, 1882–1977
Lucy, Sean, b. 1931
Lynch, Brion

Lynch, Patricia, 1898–1972
Lynd, Robert Wilson, 1879–1949
Lyons, Francis Steward Leland,
   1923–83
Lysaght, Edward, 1763–1810
Lysaght, Sidney Royse, 1860–
   1941
Lytton, Lady Rosina (née
   Wheeler), 1802–82

McAllister, Alexander (Henry
   Alexander; Anthony P.
   Wharton; Lynn Brock), 1877–
   1944
MacArdle, Dorothy, 1889–1958
McAuley, James, b. 1935
McCabe, Eugene, b. 1930
McCann, John b. 1905
McCann, Michael Joseph,
   1824–83
MacCarthy, Denis Florence,
   1817–82
McCarthy, Justin, 1830–1912
MacConMara, Donnchadh
   Ruadh, 1715–1810
McCormack, W. J.; see Maxton,
   Hugh
Macready, William, 1753–1829
McCurtin, Hugh, c. 1680–1755
MacDaibheid, Diarmaid, b. 1947
MacDonagh, Donagh, 1912–68
MacDonagh, Thomas, 1878–
   1916
MacDonogh, Patrick, 1902–61
McDowell, Robert Brendan, b.
   1914
MacEntee, Marie, b. 1922
McFadden, Hugh
McFadden, Roy, b. 1922
MacGahern, John, b. 1935
MacGauran, Hugh
McGowran, Jack, 1918–73

McGee, Thomas D'Arcy, 1825–68
MacGill, Patrick, 1891–1960
MacGreevy, Thomas, 1893–1967
McGuckian, Medbh, b. 1950
McGuinness, Frank, b. 1953
McGurk, Tom, b. 1946
McHugh, Roger, b. 1908
McIntyre, Tom, b. 1946
Macken, Walter, 1915–67
McKenna, Stephen, 1872–1934
Macklin, Charles, ?1697–1797
McLaughlin, Tom
McLaverty, Bernard, b. 1942
McLaverty, Michael, b. 1907
MacLiammóir, Micheál (Alfred Willmore), 1899–1978
MacLysaght, Edward, 1887–1986
MacMahon, Bryan, b. 1909
MacManus, Francis, 1909–65
MacManus, Seamus, 1861–1960
McNally, Leonard, 1752–1820
McNamara, Brinsley (John Weldon), 1890–1963
MacNamara, Francis, 1884–1916
MacNamara, Gerald (Harry Marrow), 1866–1938
MacNeice, Louis, 1907–63
McNeill, Janet, b. 1907
McNulty, Edward Matthew, 1856–1943
MacSwiney, Owen, ?1675–1754
Magee, Heno, b. 1939
Magee, William Kirkpatrick; see Eglinton, John
Maginn, William, 1793–1842
Mahaffy, Sir John Pentland, 1839–1919
Mahon, Derek, b. 1941
Mahony, Francis Sylvester; (Father Prout), 1831–85
Malone, Andrew E.; see Byrne, Laurence Patrick
Malone, Edmund, 1741–1812
Mangan, James Clarence, 1803–1849
Mannin, Ethel, b. 1900
Manning, Mary, b. 1906
Marsh, Narcissus, 1638–1713
Marcus, David, b. 1926
Martin, Violet Florence (the 'Ross' of Somerville and Ross), 1862–1915
Martyn, Edward, 1859–1923
Mathews, Tom, b. 1945
Matthews, Aidan Carl, b. 1956
Maturin, Charles Robert, 1782–1824
Maxwell, Constantia, 1886–1962
Maxwell, D(esmond), E. S.
Maxwell, William Hamilton, 1792–1850
Mayne, Rutherford (Samuel Waddell), 1878–1967
Maxton, Hugh (W. J. McCormack), b. 1947
Merriman, Brian, 1749–1805
Mercier, Vivian
Meyer, Kuno, 1858–1919
Michael, Friar, ?–?
Milligan, Alice L., 1865–1953
Milliken, Richard Alfred, 1767–1815
Milne, Ewart, b. 1903
Mitchel, John, 1815–75
Mitchell, Susan Langstaff, 1866–1926
Molloy, Charles, ?b. 1690–1767
Molloy, Michael J., b. 1917
Molyneux, William, 1656–98
Montague, John, b. 1929
Montgomery, Leslie A.; see Doyle, Lynn C., 1873–1961
Moore, Brian, b. 1921
Moore, George Augustus, 1852–1933

Moore, Thomas, 1779–1852
Moran, Michael (Zozimus), 1794–1846
Morgan, Lady Sydney (née Owenson), ?1785–1859
Morrow, Harry; see MacNamara, Gerald
Morrow, John, b. 1930
Mozeen, Thomas, d. 1768
Muirchi, Saint, fl. 7th century
Muldoon, Paul, b. 1951
Mulholland, Rosa (Lady Gilbert), 1841–1921
Mulkerns, Val, b. 1925
Murdoch, Iris, b. 1920
Murphy, Aidan, b. 1952
Murphy, Arthur, 1727–1805
Murphy, Donal, b. 1929
Murphy, Hayden, b. 1945
Murphy, Michael J., b. 1913
Murphy, Richard, b. 1927
Murphy, Thomas, b. 1936
Murray, John Fisher, 1811–65
Murray, Paul, b. 1947
Murray, T. C., 1873–1959

na gCopaleen, Myles (Flann O'Brien); see O'Nolan, Brian
Nally, Thomas Henry, 1869–1932
ni Chonaill, Eibhlin Dhubh, ?1743–1800
Noonan, Gillian, b. 1937
Noonan, Robert; see Tressell, Robert, 1870–1911
Norcott, William, ?b. 1770–1820
Norton, Caroline Elizabeth Sarah, the Hon, 1798–1877
ni Chuilleanian, Eilean, b. 1942

O'Brien, Charlotte Grace, 1845–1909
O'Brien, Conor Cruise (Donat O'Donnell), b. 1917
O'Brien, Edna, b. 1932
O'Brien, Gearold, b. 1955
O'Brien, Kate, 1897–1974
O'Brien, Kate Cruise, b. 1948
O'Brien, William, 1852–1928
O'Brien, Flann (na gCopaleen, Myles); see O'Nolan, Brian
O'Bruadair, Daibhi (David), c. 1625–98
O'Byrne, Dermot (Arnold Bax), 1883–1953
O'Cadhain, Mairtin, 1906–70
O'Callaghan, Turlough, 1670–1738
O'Casey, Sean (John Casey), 1884–1964
O'Clery, Michael, 1575–1643
O'Conaire, Padraic, 1883–1928
O'Connell, Charles C.
O'Connor, Frank (Michael Francis O'Donovan), 1903–66
O'Connor, Ulick, b. 1929
O'Criadain, Sean, b. 1930
O'Criomhthain, Tomas, 1856–1937
O'Curraoin, Sean, b. 1942
O'Curry, Eugene, 1796–1862
O'Daley, Aengus, d. 1617
O'Daley, John, 1800–78
O'Direain, Mairtin, b. 1910
O'Donnell, Donat; see O'Brien, Conor Cruise
O'Donnell, John Francis, 1837–74
O'Donnell, Peadar, b. 1893
O'Donoghue, David James, 1866–1917
O'Donoghue, John, 1900–64
O'Donovan, Gerald (Jeremiah O'Donovan), 1871–
O'Donovan, John, 1809–61

Parameters of Irish Literature in English 41

O'Donovan, John (Purcell), b. 1921
O'Duffy, Eimar, 1893–1935
O'Duinnin, Padraig (Father Patrick Dineen), 1860–1934
O'Faolain, Eileen (née Gould)
O'Faolain, Julia, b. 1933
O'Faolain, Sean, b. 1900
O'Farachain, Riobeard; see Farren, Robert
O'Flaherty, Liam, 1897–1985
O'Flanagan, Theophilus, 1762–1814
O'Flynn, Criostoir, b. 1927
Ogle, George, 1739–1814
O'Grady, Desmond, b. 1935
O'Grady, Standish Hayes, 1832–1915
O'Grady, Standish James, 1846–1928
O'Growney, Father Eugene, 1863–99
O'Halloran, Sylvester, 1728–1807
O'Hanrahan, Michael, ?–1916
O'Hanlon, Henry B., ?–?
O'hEigearthough, Sean Sairseal (Sean O'Hegarty), 1917–67
O'Higgins, Thomas, ? fl. 1680
O'Uanachain, Micheal, b. 1944
O'hUiginn, Tadhg Dall, 1550–91
Q'Keefe, John, 1747–1833
O'Kelly, Seumas, ?1881–1918
O'Laoghaire, Peadar (Father Peadar O'Leary), 1839–1920
O'Leary, Con, 1887–1958
O'Leary, Eileen, 1831–89
O'Leary, John, 1830–1907
O'Leary, Margaret, ??fl. 1935
O'Looney, Brian, 1827–1901
O'Luing, Sean, b. 1917
O'Muirgcadhagh, Reamoan, b. 1938
O'Muirthile, Liam, b. 1950
O'Neill, Eugene (Gladstone), 1888–1953
O'Neill, Joseph, 1886–1953
O'Neill, Maire; see Allgood, Molly
O'Neill, Mary Devenport, b. 1893
O'Nolan, Brian (na gCopaleen, Myles and Flann O'Brien), 1911–66
O'Rathaille, Aodhagan (Egan O'Rahilly), 1670–1726
O'Reilly, John Boyle, 1844–90
O'Riordain, Sean, 1916–77
O'Riordan, Conal Holmes O'Connel, 1874–1948
O'Tuairisc, Eoghan, b. 1919
Ormsby, Frank, b. 1947
Orr, James, 1770–1816
O'Shaughnessy, Arthur, 1844–81
O'Suilleabhain, Diarmaid, b. 1932
O'Suilleabhain, Eogan (Owen Roe O'Sullivan), ?1748–84
O'Suilleabhain, Muiris (Maurice O'Sullivan), 1904–50
O'Sullivan, D. J., b. 1906
O'Sullivan, Seamus (James Sullivan Starkey), 1879–1958
O'Tuama, Finin, b. 1951
Otway, Rev. Caesar, 1780–1842
Oulton, Walley Chamberlain, 1750–1820
Owenson, Sydney; see Lady Morgan

Pakenham, Thomas, b. 1933
Parker, Stewart, b. 1941
Parnell, Anna Catherine (Fanny), 1854–82
Parnell, Rev. Thomas, 1679–1718
Patrick, Saint, d. c. 490

Paulin, Tom, b. 1949
Payne, Basil, b. 1928
Pearse, Patrick, 1879–1916
Persse, Isabella Augusta; see
  Gregory, Lady
Peters, Anne
Petrie, George, 1789/90–1865
Philbin, William
Philips, William, d. 1734
Pilkington, Laetitia, 1712–50
Pim, Sheila, b. 1909
Plunkett, Edward John Moreton
  Drax, 18th Baron Dunsany;
  see Dunsany, Lord, 1878–1959
Plunkett, James (James Plunkett
  Kelly), b. 1920
Plunkett, Joseph Mary, 1887–
  1916
Pollock; J. H. see An Pilibin
Power, Marguerite; see
  Blessington, Countess of
Power, Richard, 1928–70
Power, William Grattan Tyrone,
  1797–1841
Praeger, Robert Lloyd, 1865–
  1939
Prout, Father; see Mahony,
  Francis Sylvester
Purcell, Patrick Joseph, b. 1914
Purdon, Katherine, ?–?

Quigley, Hugh, 1818–83

Rafroidi, Patrick
Raftery, Anthony, c. 1784–1835
Ray, R. J. (Brophy, R. J.),
  ?1865–?
Read, Charles Anderson,
  1841–78
Reddin, Kenneth Sheils; see
  Sarr, Kenneth, 1895–1967
Reid, Forrest, 1876–1947
Reynolds, Lorna

Robertson, Olivia, b. 1917
Robinson, Esmé Stuart Lennox,
  1886–1958
Roche, Regina Mary, 1764–1845
Rodgers, William Robert,
  1909–69
Rolleston, Thomas William,
  1857–1920
Rooney, Padraig
Rooney, Philip, 1907–62
Ros, Amanda M'Kittrick (née
  Anna Margaret M'Kittrick),
  1860–1939
Ross, Martin (the 'Ross' of
  Somerville and Ross); see
  Martin, Violet Florence
Rossa, Jeremiah O'Donovan,
  1831–1915
Rowley, Richard (William S.
  Richard), 1877–1947
Russell, George William ('AE'),
  1867–1935
Russell, Sir William Howard,
  1821–1907
Ryan, Cornelius, 1920–74
Ryan, Frederick, 1876–1913
Ryan, Richard, b. 1949
Ryves, Elizabeth, 1750–97

Salkeld, Blanaid, 1880–1959
Savage, Marmion, 1803–72
Sayers, Peig, 1873–1958
Scotus Eriugena, Johannes, ?b.
  810–887
Scully, Maurice, b. 1952
Shanihan, Eileen, b. 1901
Share, Bernard, b. 1930
Shaw, George Bernard, 1856–
  1950
Sheehan, Canon Patrick
  Augustine, 1852–1913
Sheehy-Skeffington, Francis,
  1878–1916

Sheil, Richard Lawlor, 1791–1857
Sheridan, Frances, 1724–66
Sheridan, John D., b. 1903
Sheridan, Niall Joseph, b. 1912
Sheridan, Richard Brinsley, 1751–1816
Sheridan, Thomas, 1719–88
Shiels, George, 1886–1949
Shorter (née Sigerson), Mrs Clement, 1866–1918
Sigerson, Dora; see Shorter, Mrs Clement
Sigerson, George, 1836–1925
Simmons, James, b. 1933
Sirr, Peter
Sloane, Sir Hans, 1660–1753
Smith, Michael, b. 1942
Smith, Paul, ?b. 1920
Smith, Sydney Bernard
Smithson, Annie, 1873–1948
Smyth, Gerard, b. 1951
Smythe, Colin, b. 1942
Somerville and Ross; see Somerville, Edith and Martin, Violet
Somerville, Edith Anna Oenone (the 'Somerville' of Somerville and Ross), 1858–1949
Southerne, Thomas, 1660–1746
Spenser, Edmund, ?1552–99
Speranza; see Wilde, Lady
Stacpoole, Henry de Vere, 1863–1951
Stanford, William Bedell, 1910–85
Stanyhurst, Richard, 1547–1618
Starkey, James Sullivan; see O'Sullivan, Seumas
Starkie, Enid Mary, ?1899–1970
Starkie, Walter Fitzgerald, 1894–1976
Steele, Sir Richard, 1672–1729

Stephens, James, 1880–1950
Sterne, Rev. Laurence, 1713–68
Stoker, Bram (Abraham Stoker), 1847–1912
Stokes, Whitley, 1830–1909
Strong, Eithne (née O'Connell), b. 1923
Strong, Leonard Alfred George, 1898–1958
Stuart, Francis, b. 1902
Sullivan, Timothy, 1827–1914*
Sweeney, Matthew, b. 1952
Swift, Jonathan, 1667–1745
Synge, John Millington, 1871–1909
Tate, Nahum, 1652–1715
Taylor, Geoffrey, 1890–1956
Thompson, Sam (Samuel), 1916–65
Thomson, David, b. 1914
Thurston, Katherine Cecil (nee Madden), 1875–1911
Todd, James Henthorne, Rev, 1805–69
Todhunter, John, 1839–1916
Toland, John, 1669–1722
Tomelty, Joseph, b. 1911
Tone, Theobald Wolfe, 1763–98
Torrens, Robert, 1780–1864
Tracy, Honor, b. 1913
Treacy, Maura, b. 1930
Trench, Herbert, 1865–1923
Trench, Melasina, 1768–1837
Trench, Rt Rev Richard Chenevix, 1807–80
Trench, William Steuart, 1808–72
Tressell, Robert (Robert Noonan), 1870–1911
Trevor, William (Trevor Cox), b. 1928
Trollope, Anthony, 1815–82
Tuohy, Frank

Tynan, Katherine; see Hinkson, Katherine Tynan, 1861–1931
Tyrrell, Robert Yelverton, 1844–1914

Ussher (Percival) Arland, b. 1899
Ussher, James, 1581–1656

Verschoyle, Moira, b. 1904
Voynich, Ethel Lilian (née Boole), 1867–?1947

Waddell, Helen, 1889–1965
Waddell, Samuel; see Mayne, Rutherford, 1878–1967
Walker, Joseph Cooper, 1761–1810
Wall, Mervyn (Eugene Welply), b. 1908
Waller, John Francis, 1810–94
Walsh, Edward, 1805–50
Walsh, Maurice, 1879–1964
Ware, Sir James, 1594–1666
Watson, C. J.
Watters, Eugene, b. 1919
Watters, Loughlin
Webb, Alfred John, 1834–1908
Weber, Richard, b. 1932
Weekes, Charles, 1867–1946
Welch, Robert, b. 1947
Welcome, John (J. N .H. Brennan), b. 1914
Weldon, John; see MacNamara, Brinsley
Welply, Eugene; see Wall, Mervyn
West, Anthony C., b. 1910
Wharton, Anthony P.; see McAllister, Alister and Brock, Lynn
Whelan, John; see O'Faolain, Sean

White, Jack (William John), 1920–80
White, Joseph Blanco, 1775–1841
White, Terence de Vere, b. 1912
White, Terence Hanbury, 1906–64
Whyte, Samuel, 1733–1811
Wilde, Lady Jane Francesca 'Speranza' (née Elgee); ?1820 or 1826–96
Wilde, Oscar Fingall O'Flahertie Wills, 1856–1900
Wilde, Sir William Robert Willis, 1815–76
Wilkins, Maurice, 1885–?
Wilks, Robert, c. 1665–1732
Williams, Richard D'Alton, 1822–62
Williamson, Bruce, b. 1922
Wilson, A. P., ?1880–?
Wilson, Charles Henry, ?fl. 1782
Wilson, R. N. D., 1899–1953
Wingfield, Lewis Strange, the Hon, 1842–91
Wingfield, Sheila, Viscountess Powerscourt, b. 1906
Wolfe, Charles, 1791–1825
Wood-Martin, William Gregory, 1847–1917
Woods, Macdara, b. 1942
Wykham, Helen, ?b. 1933

Yeats, Jack Butler (William Bird), 1871–1957
Yeats, John Butler, 1839–1922
Yeats, William Butler, 1865–1939
Young, Augustus, b. 1943
Young, Ella, 1865–1951

Zozimus; see Moran, Michael.